Table of contents

Jalapeño Poppers 4

Keto Chicken Salad... 6

Keto Beef with Zucchini... 9

Keto Guacamole.. 11

Chicken Quesadillas 13

Keto Roasted Zucchini... 15

Keto Relleno Taco Casserole 17

Keto Zucchini Nachos 19

Keto Meatloaf... 21

Tuna salad plate 23

Lemon Butter Smoked Salmon... 25

Egg and crab plate.. 27

Baked omelet with bacon 29

Mushroom omelet... 31

Salmon stuffed avocados... 33

Keto Quesadillas 35

Keto Cheesy Mexican Low Carb Skillet 37

Swedish Meatballs... 39

Mushroom Omelet 41

Chicken with herb butter 43

Pork chops with blue cheese 45

Hearty Keto chili.. 47

Creamy Mushroom Chicken.. 49

Cauliflower Mac and Cheese.. 51

Chicken and Creamy Dill sauce.. 53

Sheet pan Burgers with bacon and jalapenos 56

Chicken with Bacon and Ranch 58

Chicken Philly Cheesesteak bowl 60

Keto Kung Pao Chicken... 62

Fish fingers with Chimichurri mayo.. 65

Filipino Skirt steak with Cauliflower fried rice 68

Coconut Curry Chicken.. 71

Crab Cakes.. 73

Keto Lasagna from Scratch... 75

Omelet pizza.. 78

Hassleback Chicken Caprese 80

Italian Chicken Cacciatore 82

Bacon Cheeseburger Soup 85

Chicken Satay with Peanut Sauce 88

Spicy Ramen Bowl 91

Vegetarian Tikka Masala 93

Vegetarian Greek Collard Wraps 96

Beef and Broccoli Bowls with Sunshine Sauce 98

Loaded Cauliflower Mash 101

Salmon Gremolata with vegetables 103

Cauliflower Bibimbap 105

Avocado Breakfast Burgers 108

Taco Bites 110

Fried Chicken Tenders 112

Seared Scallops and Cauliflower Rice Risotto 115

Jalapeño Poppers

Prep Time:	5 minutes	Calories:	78.8
Cook Time:	10 minutes	Fat (g):	27.7
Total Time:	15 minutes	Protein (g):	19.2
Servings:	4	Net carbs:	1.9

Ingredients:

- Cheddar cheese   1 (16-ounce) package
- jalapeño peppers   6
- slices pre-cooked bacon   12
- Non-stick cooking spray

Instructions:

1. Preheat the oven to broil.
2. Seed and halve the jalapeños. Set aside.
3. Cut cheese into 12 slices that are long enough to fit inside the jalapeño halves; insert the cheese into the jalapeño halves.
4. Wrap the jalapeño halves with the bacon slices. Secure each with a toothpick. Place on the prepared baking sheet.
5. Broil (watching closely) for 5 minutes initially. Return to oven and broil up to an additional 5 minutes. Bacon needs to be brown.

Keto Chicken Salad

Prep Time:	15 minutes	Calories:	446
Cook Time:	10 minutes	Fat (g):	41
Total Time:	25 minutes	Protein (g):	29
Servings:	4	Net carbs:	12

Ingredients:

<u>For the fajita seasoning:</u>

- chili powder .... 2 teaspoons
- onion powder .... 1 teaspoon
- smoked paprika .... 1 teaspoon
- salt .... 1/2 teaspoon
- cumin .... 1 teaspoons
- garlic powder .... 1 teaspoon

<u>For the fajitas:</u>

- olive oil .... 2 tablespoons
- juice from 1 lime
- chicken breasts (pounded to even thickness) ... 2 medium
- ground mustard .... 1/2 teaspoon
- butter divided .... 2 tablespoons
- bell peppers (sliced into strips) ... 4 medium
- red onion (sliced into strips) ...... 1 medium
- butter lettuce leaves 2-3
- romaine lettuce leaves 2-3

For serving:

- sliced avocado

Instructions:

1. Take a medium sized bowl and add all the seasoning ingredients to it. Mix well.

2. Now take a resealable bag and add lime juice, 2tbsp. olive oil, chicken and 2 tsp. seasoning mixture to it.

3. Seal the bag and let the chicken marinate.

4. Add 1 tbsp. butter in a pan and heat it. Add onions and cook for about 5 minutes.

5. Now add bell peppers and remaining fajita seasoning to the pan and cook for about 4 minutes. Once they are cooked, remove from the pan and transfer to a plate. Set aside.

6. Melt the remaining butter on the pan and add chicken to it. Cook for about 5 minutes or until the chicken turns brown.

7. Arrange lettuce in a plate and place chicken over them. Top with the bell peppers and sliced avocado. You can also top it with any topping you want.

8. Serve and enjoy!

Keto Beef with Zucchini

Prep Time:	5 minutes	Calories:	272
Cook Time:	25 minutes	Fat (g):	17.5
Total Time:	30 minutes	Protein (g):	22
Servings:	6	Net carbs:	5.6

Ingredients:

- zucchini (sliced and quartered)   2 medium
- Salsa   10 ounces
- chili powder   1 tablespoon
- ground cumin   1 teaspoon
- ground beef   1 1/2 pounds
- garlic minced   2 cloves
- salt   1 teaspoon
- black pepper   1/2 teaspoon
- red pepper flakes (crushed)   1/4 teaspoon
- onion powder   1/2 teaspoon

Instructions:

1. Heat a pan over medium heat. Add garlic, ground beef, salt, and pepper to the pan and cook it until it is brown.
2. Add the remaining spices along with tomatoes. Cook for 10 more minutes.
3. Now add zucchini to the pan and close the lid. Cook for about 10 minutes.
4. Remove from the pan and serve.
5. Enjoy!

Keto Guacamole

Prep Time:	10 minutes	Calories:	300
Cook Time:	0 minutes	Fat (g):	25
Total Time:	10 minutes	Protein (g):	4
Servings:	2	Net carbs:	5

Ingredients:

• ripe avocado	1 medium
• lime juice	1/2 teaspoon
• lime with the peel on, diced	1 slice
• onion powder	1/2 teaspoon
• garlic powder	1/2 teaspoon
• Cayenne pepper	to taste
• cherry tomatoes, chopped	2
• cilantro, chopped	1 Tablespoon
• Salt	to taste

Instructions:

1. Mash the avocados.
2. Take a small sized bowl and add lime juice, mashed avocados and lime pieces to it. Mix well.
3. Add all the remaining ingredients to the bowl and mix again.
4. You can serve this guacamole alone or with any other dish.
5. Enjoy!

Chicken Quesadillas

Prep Time:	5 minutes	Calories:	105
Cook Time:	2 minutes	Fat (g):	7.7
Total Time:	7 minutes	Protein (g):	7.5
Servings:	6	Net carbs:	3.9

Ingredients:

- low carb tortilla   1 (10-inch)
- shredded cheddar cheese   1/2 cup
- shredded cooked chicken   1/2 cup
- chopped avocado   1/4 cup
- fresh small jalapeño chile peppers   2
- homemade salsa   1/2 cup
- Nonstick cooking spray

Instructions:

1. Seed and thinly slice the jalapeño chile peppers. Lightly coat one side of a tortilla with cooking spray. Sprinkle shredded cheese on the unsprayed side of the tortilla.
2. Top with chicken, avocado and jalapeño slices.
3. Carefully fold the tortilla over the filling. Use a griddle or iron skillet. Heat the skillet before placing the tortilla in it.
4. Cook quesadilla for 1 to 2 minutes on each side until lightly browned and cheese is melted. Cut into 6 wedges.
5. Serve with fresh salsa.

Keto Roasted Zucchini

Prep Time:	5 minutes	Calories:	267
Cook Time:	25 minutes	Fat (g):	18.7
Total Time:	30 minutes	Protein (g):	4
Servings:	4	Net carbs:	6.5

Ingredients:

- medium zucchini (diced)   3-4
- olive oil   2 tablespoons
- cayenne pepper   1/8 teaspoon
- salt and pepper   to taste
- chili powder   1/2 teaspoon
- garlic powder   1/2 teaspoon
- cotija cheese (crumbled)
- lime juice
- fresh cilantro, for garnish (optional)

Instructions:

1. Preheat your oven to 425 degrees.
2. Mix all the ingredients except lime juice, cilantro, and cheese in a bowl.
3. Spread this mixture on a baking sheet lined with parchment paper. Roast for about 25 minutes.
4. Once the zucchini turns brown, remove the baking sheet from oven and sprinkle with cilantro, lime juice, and cotija cheese.
5. Serve and enjoy!

Keto Relleno Taco Casserole

Prep Time:	5 minutes	Calories:	426
Cook Time:	20 minutes	Fat (g):	28
Total Time:	25 minutes	Protein (g):	32
Servings:	4	Net carbs:	8

Ingredients:

For the Ground Beef

- taco seasoning   1 tablespoon
- ground beef   1 pound

For the Topping

- Eggs   2
- diced green chilis   7 ounces
- Flour   2 tablespoons
- Mexican Blend Cheese shredded 1 cup
- Milk   3/4 cup
- salt   to taste

Instructions:

1. Heat a pan over medium heat. Add ground beef to the pan and cook it until it is brown.
2. Add taco seasoning to the pan and mix well.
3. Take an 8x8 glass pan and add the ground beef to it.
4. Whisk together milk, flour, and eggs in a medium sized bowl and add cheese along with green chilies to it. Mix well.
5. Pour the cheesy topping over the ground beef. Cook it in a pre-heated oven for about 20 minutes.
6. Once done, remove from the oven and serve.
7. Enjoy!

Keto Zucchini Nachos

Prep Time:	10 minutes	Calories:	116
Cook Time:	18 minutes	Fat (g):	8
Total Time:	28 minutes	Protein (g):	9
Servings:	8	Net carbs:	2.3

Ingredients:

- No Bean Low Carb Chili   ½ cups
- mozzarella cheese (grated)   1/2 cup
- olive oil   2 to 3 tablespoons
- zucchini thinly sliced   1 large
- sharp cheddar cheese (grated)   3/4 cup

Instructions:

1. Preheat your oven to 350 degrees.
2. Place zucchini slices in a greased baking sheet and brush them with olive oil.
3. Bake zucchini for about 7 minutes and then remove from oven.
4. Top the zucchini with low carb chili and then cheeses.
5. Bake again for about 10 minutes or until the cheese is melted.
6. Let the nachos cool and then serve.
7. Enjoy!

Keto Meatloaf

Prep Time:	5 minutes	Calories:	507
Cook Time:	20 minutes	Fat (g):	33
Total Time:	25 minutes	Protein (g):	29
Servings:	4	Net carbs:	4.7

Ingredients:

- ground beef   2 lbs
- egg   1
- chunky salsa   1 cup
- taco seasoning   1 package
- pork rind flour (fine crumbs)   1 cup
- grated cheddar cheese   1 cup

Instructions:

1. Take a medium sized bowl and add hamburger, rind flour, egg, and a cup of salsa. Mix well.
2. Preheat your oven to 350 degrees.
3. Divide the meat mixture and cheese into two halves.
4. Add one half of the meat mixture to a bread loaf and press well. Pour one half of the cheese over it.
5. Add remaining meat mixture and bake for about one hour.
6. Pour the remaining cheese into the bread pan and bake for another six minutes.
7. Serve warm with cream cheese and chopped tomatoes.
8. Enjoy!

Tuna salad plate

Prep Time:	5 minutes	Calories	482
Cook Time:	10 minutes	Fat (g)	38
Total Time:	15 minutes	Protein (g)	26
Servings:	2	Net Carbs (g)	2

Ingredients:

- Tuna in olive oil   10 oz.
- Eggs   4
- Avocado   1
- Baby spinach   2 oz.
- Salt and pepper   to taste
- Mayonnaise   ½ cup

Instructions:

1. Boil the eggs and slice them into half once done.
2. In a plate, place the eggs, avocado, and tuna.
3. Drop-in some mayo and season with salt and pepper to serve!

Lemon Butter Smoked Salmon

Prep Time:	5 minutes	Calories	573
Cook Time:	25 minutes	Fat (g)	49
Total Time:	30 minutes	Protein (g)	31
Servings:	6	Net Carbs (g)	1

Ingredients:

- olive oil   1 tbsp.
- salmon   2 lbs
- ground black pepper   1 tsp
- butter   7 oz.
- lemon   1
- sea salt   1 tsp

Instructions:

1. The oven is to be preheated to 400°F.
2. Slick a baking tray with olive oil.
3. Place the salmon (flesh up) in the oiled baking dish.
4. Season generously with salt and pepper.
5. Cut thin slices of the lemon to place them over the salmon.
6. Cover with half of the butter in thin slices.
7. Keep it in the mid-section and bake for half an hour.
8. To check if the salmon is cooked or not, try flaking with a fork—if it does so quickly, it's cooked!
9. Add in the leftover butter and cook again for a couple of minutes.
10. Pull out the tray, squeeze some lemon juice, and serve!

Egg and crab plate

Prep Time:	5 minutes	Calories	550
Cook Time:	10 minutes	Fat (g)	48
Total Time:	15 minutes	Protein (g)	22
Servings:	2	Net Carbs (g)	4

Ingredients:

• Eggs	4
• Crabmeat	12 oz. canned
• Avocados	2
• Cottage cheese	½ cup
• Baby spinach	1½ oz.
• Olive oil	2 tbsp.
• Salt and pepper	To taste

Instructions:

1. Boil the eggs (as you like them) and slice them up once done.
2. In a plate, place the eggs in, crab meat, spinach, avocado, and cottage cheese.
3. Season with some salt and pepper, and you can also add some chili flakes for a little kick.
4. Drizzle some olive oil and serve!

Baked omelet with bacon

Prep Time:	5 minutes	Calories	380
Cook Time:	20 minutes	**Fat (g)**	38
Total Time:	25 minutes	**Protein (g)**	11
Servings:	2	**Net Carbs (g)**	1

Ingredients:

- Butter   3 oz.
- Eggs   4
- Fresh spinach   2 oz.
- Bacon   5 oz.
- Salt and pepper   to taste

Instructions:

1. In a skillet, add some butter and fry the bacon. Take it out and in the same pan, add the spinach and sauté it.
2. In a bowl, crack the eggs and start whisking. Once it's foamy, add the bacon, spinach and the fat.
3. Sprinkle some salt and pepper and stir it again.
4. Cover a baking tray with some cooking spray and pour the mixture in it.
5. Place the tray inside a pre-heated oven (at 390 F) and bake.
6. Cool it down and serve with bread if you want!

Mushroom omelet

Prep Time:	5 minutes	Calories	517
Cook Time:	10 minutes	Fat (g)	44
Total Time:	15 minutes	Protein (g)	26
Servings:	1	Net Carbs (g)	5

Ingredients:

- butter, for frying   1 oz.
- eggs   3
- yellow onion, chopped   ¼

- shredded cheese   1 oz.
- Salt and pepper   to taste
- large mushrooms, sliced   4

Instructions:

1. Whip eggs in a bowl until they're smooth and frothy. Don't forget to add salt and pepper.

2. Melt the butter in the pan to fry the mushrooms and onions. Fry them and stir them until they are tender. Then pour in the egg mixture over the veggies.

3. As the omelet cooks, but still has a little raw mixture on top, drizzle some cheese over the egg.

4. Fold the omelet with its other half using a spatula and when you see a golden-brown color approaching it, slide the omelet on to a plate.

Salmon stuffed avocados

Prep Time:	5 minutes	Calories	438
Cook Time:	0 minutes	Fat (g)	36
Total Time:	5 minutes	Protein (g)	26
Servings:	2	Net Carbs (g)	3

Ingredients:

- smoked salmon   6 oz.
- avocados   2
- salt and pepper   to taste
- mayonnaise   ¾ cup
- lemon juice (optional)   2 tbsp.

Instructions:

1. Scoop the pit of the avocado.
2. Add a big blotch of crème Fraiche or mayonnaise into the avocado and add smoked salmon to it.
3. Use salt for seasoning and add a little lemon juice for extra flavor.

Keto Quesadillas

Prep Time:	15 minutes	Calories:	246
Cook Time:	15 minutes	Fat (g):	21
Total Time:	30 minutes	Protein (g):	13
Servings:	3	Net carbs:	4

Ingredients:

For Tortillas:

- Eggs   2
- Egg Whites   2
- Cream Cheese   6 oz.

- Salt   ½ tsp.
- Psyllium Husk   1 ½ tsp.
- Coconut Flour   1 tbsp.

For the filling:

- Olive Oil   1 tbsp.
- Mexican Cheese   5 oz.
- Spinach   1 oz.

Instructions:

1. Beat the eggs and the egg whites using an electric mixer. Add in the cream cheese in increments until the entire mixture reaches a smooth consistency.
2. Combine the husk, salt and flour in a bowl. Add this mixture to the egg and cheese mixture.
3. Layout a piece of baking paper onto a baking tray and spread your tortilla mixture onto it in your desired form. Bake the tortillas in a preheated oven at 400 F for 5 to 10 minutes (until they appear brown).
4. Place a tortilla in a medium skillet with olive oil and cook it over a medium flame. Add in the filling followed by another tortilla to form it into a quesadilla. Heat on both ends for 3 minutes.

Keto Cheesy Mexican Low Carb Skillet

A blend of all your favorite South Western flavors.

Prep Time:	10 minutes	Calories:	556
Cook Time:	20 minutes	Fat (g):	36
Total Time:	30 minutes	Protein (g):	30
Servings:	4	Net carbs:	8

Ingredients:

• Bell Pepper	½
• Avocado Oil	1 tbsp.
• Ground Beef	1 pound
• White Onion	1/2
• Can Green Chilies	4 oz.
• Taco Seasoning	3 tbsp.
• Roma Tomatoes	2
• Cauliflower Rice	12 ounces
• Avocado (diced)	1
• Jalapeno (sliced)	As needed
• Sour Cream	As needed
• Cilantro	As needed
• Mexican Cheese	1 cup

Instructions:

1. Take a large iron cast skillet and heat oil in it over a high flame.
2. Once hot, add in the beef and cook until brown.
3. To the same pan, add in the bell pepper, taco seasoning, onion and cook for an additional 3 minutes.
4. Add in the green chilies, tomatoes and cauliflower rice. Cook this assembly for 5 minutes, or until liquid has evaporated.
5. Cover with cheese and heat until melted.
6. Top with jalapeno, cilantro and avocado.

Swedish Meatballs

Prep Time:	10 minutes	Calories:	544
Cook Time:	20 minutes	Fat (g):	46
Total Time:	30 minutes	Protein (g):	28
Servings:	6	Net carbs (g):	1

Ingredients:

- Ground pork   1 lb

- Ground chuck — 1 lb
- Zucchini grated — 1 cup
- Egg — 1
- All-purpose seasoning — 1 teaspoon
- Salt — ¼ teaspoon
- Butter — 2 tablespoons
- Chicken broth — 1 cup
- Mustard — 1 tablespoon
- Heavy cream — ¾ cup

Instructions:

1. Crush the meat in a bowl.
2. Grate the zucchini.
3. Put it in the beef, crack an egg over it and sprinkle in seasoning and salt.
4. Use your hands to combine the ingredients.
5. On a cast-iron skillet, heat butter.
6. Make 18 meatballs and fry them in the butter.
7. Cook each side for 3-5 minutes.
8. Make a mixture of broth, mustard, and cream.
9. Add it in the skillet. Wait till the meatballs are done completely, and the sauce has reached desired consistency, for 5-10 minutes.
10. Enjoy!

Mushroom Omelet

Prep Time:	5 minutes	Calories:	517
Cook Time:	10 minutes	Fat (g):	44
Total Time:	15 minutes	Protein (g):	26
Servings:	1	Net carbs (g):	5

Ingredients:

- Eggs   3
- Butter   1 oz.
- Shredded cheese   1 oz.
- Yellow onion, chopped   ¼
- Mushrooms, sliced   4
- Salt and pepper   to taste

Instructions:

1. Sprinkle in salt and pepper into the cracked eggs. Mix with a fork until fluffy.
2. In the heated butter, on medium heat, sauté mushrooms and onions. Add in the eggs.
3. When the eggs almost begin to lose their rawness, spread cheese on top.
4. Fold the omelet in two with a spatula. When it becomes golden on both sides, scoop it onto a plate and enjoy!

Chicken with herb butter

Prep Time:	10 minutes	Calories:	225
Cook Time:	10 minutes	Fat (g):	19
Total Time:	20 minutes	Protein (g):	14
Servings:	4	Net carbs (g):	1

Ingredients:

- Butter   6 oz.
- Minced garlic   1
- Fresh parsley finely chopped   ¼ cup
- Lemon juice   1 teaspoon
- Salt   1 teaspoon
- Butter/olive oil   3 tablespoons
- Chicken breasts   4
- Salt and pepper   to taste

Instructions:

1. To make the herb butter, stir in all the ingredients in a small bowl.
2. Grease a large frying with butter and turn on medium heat. Sprinkle the chicken with salt and pepper. Simmer till the breasts are completely done, 165 degrees F internal temperature.
3. Serve with butter and greens!

Pork chops with blue cheese

Prep Time:	5 minutes	Calories:	193
Cook Time:	15 minutes	Fat (g):	15
Total Time:	20 minutes	Protein (g):	12
Servings:	4	Net carbs (g):	1

Ingredients:

- Blue cheese   5 oz.
- Heavy whipping cream/crème fraîch   ¾ cup
- Pork chops   4
- Salt and pepper   to taste
- Fresh green beans   7 oz.
- Butter for frying   2 tablespoons

Instructions:

1. Over medium heat, place cheese in a pot. Shape slowly or it will burn.
2. Pour in the cream and let it come to a light boil as you slightly increase the heat.
3. Sprinkle salt and pepper over chops.
4. Simmer on medium-high heat for 2-3 minutes on both sides. The meat tester should show a range of 145-160 degrees F before you let it rest inside a foil for 2-3 minutes.
5. Stir in the leftover meat juices into the cheese sauce.
6. Add salt to taste if you want. For blue cheese is already salty.
7. Simmer green beans in butter for a few minutes on medium flame. Sprinkle with salt and pepper and serve!

Hearty Keto chili

Prep Time:	5 minutes	Calories:	156
Cook Time:	25 minutes	Fat (g):	8
Total Time:	30 minutes	Protein (g):	18
Servings:	5	Net carbs (g):	4

Ingredients:

- Olive oil — 1 tablespoon
- Onion (finely chopped) — 1 small
- Green pepper (finely chopped) — 1 medium
- Garlic (finely minced) — 1 clove
- Grass-fed ground beef — 1 lb.
- Tomato paste — 3 heaped tablespoons
- Diced tomatoes — ½ cup
- Beef bone broth — 8 oz.
- Chili powder — 1 ½ teaspoons
- Cumin — 1 teaspoon
- Salt — 1 ½ teaspoons
- Pepper — ½ teaspoon

Instructions:

1. On medium flame, place a pot and drizzle olive oil. Sizzle onions and bell peppers for 1-2 minutes. Sprinkle garlic, salt and pepper, and spices.
2. Stir-fry the beef till it's brownish. Now add the tomato paste with the tomatoes and broth.
3. When it starts to bubble, reduce the heat. Keep spooning it for 20-25 minutes.
4. Garnish with cheese, sour cream, and avocado if you want. Enjoy!

Creamy Mushroom Chicken

Prep Time:	5 minutes	Calories:	334
Cook Time:	20 minutes	Fat (g):	27.3
Total Time:	25 minutes	Protein (g):	24.3
Servings:	2	Net carbs (g):	3.2

Ingredients:

- Pastured chicken cutlets   2
- Onion   1 small
- Cremona mushrooms   5
- Pink Himalayan salt   1 teaspoon
- Dried thyme   ½ teaspoon
- Unsalted butter   3 tablespoons
- Full fat canned coconut milk   ⅓ cup

Instructions:

1. Place a cast-iron skillet over medium heat while you chop your mushrooms and onions.

2. Melt 2 tablespoons of butter and slide in the chopped mushrooms, season with salt. Simmer till they gain color before adding the onions. 6 minutes will tenderize them. Take them off heat.

3. Place the seasoned (with salt and thyme) cutlets in the leftover butter. Turn each side for 5 minutes.

4. Put in the mushrooms and onions again, drizzle the coconut milk in next.

5. Boil slightly for a minute and serve flaming hot!

Cauliflower Mac and Cheese

Prep Time:	10 minutes	Calories:	393
Cook Time:	20 minutes	**Fat (g):**	33
Total Time:	30 minutes	**Protein (g):**	14
Servings:	3	**Net carbs (g):**	8

Ingredients:

- Heavy cream   8 oz.
- Sharp cheddar (Shredded)   4 oz.
- Fontana (shredded)   4 oz.
- Cream cheese   2 oz.
- Salt   1 teaspoon
- Black pepper   ½ teaspoon
- Paprika   1 ¼ teaspoons
- Head of cauliflower   1 large

Instructions:

1. Heat oven to 375F beforehand. Grease an 8×8 baking tray with butter.
2. Steam 1-inch cauliflower bits for 4-5 minutes. They should not become soft. Take them out of the heat and remove the moisture. Put aside.
3. Stir in the heavy cream, cream cheese, all the cheeses, salt, paprika, and pepper, in a pot over medium heat. Mix until no lumps are seen.
4. Toss in the steamed cauliflower, stir till it's covered by the sauce.
5. Set into a baking tray, let it bake for 20-30 minutes until baked through and golden.

Chicken and Creamy Dill sauce

Prep Time:	5 minutes	Calories:	342
Cook Time:	8 minutes	Fat (g):	26
Total Time:	13 minutes	Protein (g):	26
Servings:	4	Net carbs (g):	2

Ingredients:

- Chicken cutlets   4 (6 oz. each)
- Ground black pepper   ¼ teaspoon
- Kosher salt   1 teaspoon
- Ground paprika   1 teaspoon
- Onion powder   ½ teaspoon
- Dried oregano leaves   1 teaspoon
- Olive oil   2 tablespoons
- Mayonnaise   ½ cup
- Mashed avocado   ⅓ cup
- Fresh dill   2 tablespoons
- Fresh parsley   1 teaspoon
- Capers   1 teaspoon
- Minced garlic   1 teaspoon
- Chopped green onion   3 tablespoons
- Lemon juice   2 tablespoons
- Dill pickle juice   1 tablespoon
- White vinegar   1 tablespoon
- Olive oil   2 tablespoons
- Unsweetened almond milk 2 tablespoons
- Kosher salt   ¼ teaspoon
- Ground black pepper   ⅛ teaspoon

Instructions:

1. (for the chicken) Mix thoroughly all the spices and rub them onto the chicken.
2. Fry the chicken in oil brought to the desired temperature. Do both sides, 4 minutes each, until fully done.
3. (For the creamy dill sauce) Mix all the sauce ingredients, blend them well. No lumps should be left.
4. Sprinkle in salt and pepper to taste.
5. Decorate your plate with the chicken and creamy dill sauce.

Sheet pan Burgers with bacon and jalapenos

Prep Time:	8 minutes	Calories:	608
Cook Time:	20 minutes	**Fat (g):**	46
Total Time:	28 minutes	**Protein (g):**	42
Servings:	1	**Net carbs (g):**	4

Ingredients:

- Ground beef   24 oz.

- Kosher salt — 1 teaspoon
- Ground black pepper — ¼ teaspoon
- Garlic powder — ½ teaspoon
- Raw bacon, cut in half — 6 slices
- Onion — 4 slices
- Jalapeno, gutted and cut into rings — 2
- Pepper Jack cheese — 4 slices
- Real mayonnaise — ¼ cup
- Sriracha hot sauce — 1 tablespoon
- Worcestershire sauce — ½ teaspoon

Instructions:

1. Preheat oven to 425F
2. Knead garlic powder and salt and pepper into the beef, thoroughly.
3. Make patties of similar sizes and line them up on a baking tray, along with the bacon, jalapenos, and onion rings.
4. Set in the oven for 18 minutes.
5. Mix in the ingredients for the sauce and refrigerate until serving time.
6. Take out the baking tray and put a cheese slice on all patties
7. Turn the oven setting to high broil and place the tray back inside until cheese starts bubbling.
8. Take it out. Each burger patty will have 3 bacon, 1 onion ring, and as many jalapenos and sauce as you want.

Chicken with Bacon and Ranch

Prep Time:	5 minutes	Calories:	243
Cook Time:	25 minutes	Fat (g):	18
Total Time:	30 minutes	Protein (g):	15
Servings:	4	Net carbs (g):	2

Ingredients:

- Butter   2 tablespoons
- Homemade ranch seasoning mix   1 ½ tablespoons
- Cream cheese (softened)   4 oz.
- Heavy cream   ¼ cup
- Reduced sodium chicken broth   ⅔ cup
- Crumbled cooked Bacon   ¼ cup
- Shredded cheese   1 ½ cup
- Broccoli   4 cups
- Shredded cooked chicken   2 cups
- Shredded cheese for topping   1 ½ cup
- Crumbled cooked bacon   ½ cup

Instructions:

1. Heat oven to 350F, beforehand.
2. Grease a baking pan with butter, put on medium heat. Lower flame and stir in ranch seasoning, cream cheese, heavy cream, broth, crushed bacon and cheeses, for 5 minutes. During all this, give the broccoli steam.
3. Mix the broccoli and cooked chicken into the sauce. Top it with ½ cup of shredded cheese and crushed bacon.
4. Bake for 20 minutes, until cheese becomes golden brown and bubbly. You can broil it for a few minutes more if you want.
5. Serve steaming hot!

Chicken Philly Cheesesteak bowl

Prep Time:	10 minutes	Calories:	263
Cook Time:	15 minutes	Fat (g):	13
Total Time:	25 minutes	Protein (g):	27
Servings:	3	Net carbs (g):	5

Ingredients:

- Boneless chicken breasts   2
- Worcestershire sauce   2 tablespoons
- Onion powder   ½ teaspoon
- Garlic powder   ½ teaspoon
- Ground pepper   A pinch
- Olive oil divided   2 teaspoons
- Diced onion   ½ cup
- Diced bell pepper   ½ cup
- Minced garlic   ½ teaspoon
- Provolone cheese/queso melting cheese   3 slices

Instructions:

1. Cut chicken into thin strands and toss them into a bowl. Add Worcestershire sauce, onion powder, garlic powder, and ground pepper to season the chicken with.

2. In a 9-inch baking pan, drizzle olive oil. Fry the chicken on both sides (5 minutes for each). Dish out after cooked thoroughly.

3. Drizzle the leftover oil to the heated pan and sauté onions, garlic and bell pepper for 2-3 minutes.

4. Remove from heat and toss in the cooked chicken. Mix in the veggies and top with cheese. Put the lid on for 2-3 minutes.

5. Dig into the steaming bowls!

Keto Kung Pao Chicken

Prep Time:	15 minutes	Calories:	415
Cook Time:	12 minutes	Fat (g):	30
Total Time:	25 minutes	Protein (g):	18
Servings:	4	Net carbs (g):	8

Ingredients:

- Coconut aminos — 3 tablespoons
- Fish sauce — 1 teaspoon
- Sesame oil/avocado oil — 1 teaspoon
- Apple cider vinegar — 1 teaspoon
- Red chili flakes — ¼-½ teaspoon
- Ground ginger — ½ teaspoon
- Minced garlic — 2 cloves
- Water/chicken broth — 2-3 tablespoons
- Monk fruit — 1-2 teaspoons
- Chicken thighs (1-inch cubes) — ¾ lb
- Himalayan pink salt and black pepper — To taste
- Olive oil — 3-4 tablespoons
- Diced red bell pepper — 1
- Zucchini (sliced in two) — 1
- Dried red chili peppers/ sriracha — ½ teaspoon
- Roasted cashews — ⅔ cup
- Xanthium gum (optional) — ¼ teaspoon
- Sesame seeds and diced green onions — For garnishing

Instructions:

1. Mix in all the sauce ingredients and put sauce aside for later use.
2. Sprinkle salt and pepper as well as drizzle 1 tablespoon of the sauce onto the chicken.
3. Heat oil in a wok, over a medium high flame.
4. Sauté the chicken for 5-6 minutes.
5. Mix in the zucchini, bell peppers and dried chili pepper (or sriracha) for 2-3 minutes until everything is crisp and done. Stir in the leftover sauce and toss in the cashews. Mix well till the reaches the desired consistency.
6. Sprinkle in salt and pepper. If you want, you can add the xanthium gum to make it thicker.
7. Top it with sesame seeds and green onions. Serve!

Fish fingers with Chimichurri mayo

Prep Time:	15 minutes	Calories:	495
Cook Time:	15 minutes	Fat (g):	40.1
Total Time:	30 minutes	Protein (g):	29.6
Servings:	2	Net carbs (g):	3

Ingredients:

- Whitefish, sliced   8.8 oz.

- Egg, whisked   1 large

- Almond flour   ⅓ cup

- Sea salt   ½ teaspoon

- Onion powder   ½ teaspoon

- Garlic powder   ½ teaspoon

- Paprika   ¼ teaspoon

- Paleo mayo   ¼ cup

- Chimichurri   1 ½ tablespoons

Homemade chimichurri sauce:

- Fresh parsley   1 large bunch

- Fresh oregano   ¼ cup

- Minced garlic   4 cloves

- Red chili pepper, seeded   1 small

- Apple cider vinegar/lime juice   2 tablespoons

- Extra virgin olive oil   ½ cup

- Salt   ½ teaspoon

- Black pepper   ¼ teaspoon

Instructions:

1. Heat the oven to 210C/410F, beforehand. Whisk the egg in a plate. In another one, combine all the dry ingredients to serve as breadcrumbs.
2. Slice fish into thin finger-like strands.
3. Rub a baking sheet with butter, dip the fish slices in an egg (one by one) and then in the dry mix. Dispose of the excess.
4. Cook in oven for 6-8 minutes, flip them over and cook for 5 minutes more.
5. Blend all the chimichurri ingredients till no lump remains. Add it in the mayo to make chimichurri mayo.
6. Plate the fish with a generous serving of sauce. Enjoy!

Filipino Skirt steak with Cauliflower fried rice

Prep Time:	15 minutes	Calories:	341
Cook Time:	15 minutes	Fat (g):	17.5
Total Time:	30 minutes	Protein (g):	39
Servings:	3	Net carbs (g):	8

Ingredients:

- Skirt steak with the silver skin removed   1 lb
- Fried eggs (optional)   2 large

  Steak seasonings (best marinate overnight):
- Coconut aminos   3 tablespoons
- Coarse salt   ½ teaspoon
- Lime juice   ¼ lime
- Crushed garlic cloves   2 large
- Black pepper   to taste

  Cauliflower fried rice:
- Cauliflower rice   2 cups
- Chopped scallions (with separate green and white parts)   2-3 bulbs
- Finely chopped garlic cloves   2 small
- Ginger grated   ¼ teaspoon
- Coconut aminos   2 teaspoon
- Sesame oil   1 teaspoon
- Coarse salt   to taste

  Quick tomato sauce:
- Finely chopped, ripe tomato   1
- Finely chopped, shallots   1 ½ tablespoons
- Finely chopped, fresh parsley   2 tablespoons

- Lime juice   to taste

Instructions:

1. Make ridges in the steak, crisscrossing each other. Let it soak in the "steak seasonings" overnight for best results or refrigerate for 1-2 hours at the very least

2. Fry the steak in 1 teaspoon ghee on an already hot cast iron, for 2-3 minutes (both sides). Put it aside to settle in its own juices and ghee.

3. Heat ghee in a skillet, place white scallion parts and minced garlic after reducing the heat to medium. Add a dash of salt, wait for 10 seconds until aromatic. Stir in the rice, ginger, aminos, and sesame oil. Toss a few times to avoid extra soft rice. Add the green scallion parts after removing from heat.

4. Cut the steak into slices and dish out with rice, fried egg and a dollop of tomato sauce.

Coconut Curry Chicken

Prep Time:	5 minutes	Calories:	251
Cook Time:	25 minutes	Fat (g):	17
Total Time:	30 minutes	Protein (g):	14
Servings:	6	Net carbs (g):	8

Ingredients:

- Olive oil (divided)   2 tablespoon

- Onion (chopped)   ½ large
- Chicken breast   2 lbs
- Diced tomatoes   14.5 oz. can
- Chicken broth   ¼ cup
- Crushed garlic   4 cloves
- Curry powder   1 ½ teaspoons
- Ground ginger   2 teaspoons
- Paprika   1 teaspoon
- Sea salt   ½ teaspoon

Instructions:

1. In a large skillet, drizzle oil and simmer onions for 7-10 minutes or until they gain a darker shade, over medium flame.

2. Nudge the onions aside in the pan and on medium-high flame drizzle a tablespoon of oil. Layer the chicken in a single file and fry till 1-2 minutes on both sides. Till the outside gains color.

3. Stir in the coconut cream, diced tomatoes, chicken broth, curry powder, garlic, ginger, paprika and sea salt (to taste).

4. When the mixture starts bubbling, lower the flame and let it be for 15-20 minutes. The chicken should be tender and the sauce, the desired consistency to incorporate all the flavors.

5. Enjoy!

Crab Cakes

Prep Time:	10 minutes	Calories:	106
Cook Time:	20 minutes	Fat (g):	7
Total Time:	30 minutes	Protein (g):	9
Servings:	8	Net carbs (g):	2

Ingredients:

• Lump crab meat	1 lb
• Finely chopped onion	½ cup
• Balanced almond flour	3 tablespoons
• Egg white	¼ cup
• Mayonnaise	2 tablespoons
• Worcestershire sauce	1 teaspoon
• Mustard	1 teaspoon
• Dried parsley	1 tablespoon
• Seafood seasoning	1 tablespoon
• Olive oil divided	2 tablespoons

Instructions:

1. Drizzle oil in a heated skillet, on medium flame. Fry the onions until they darken, for 10 minutes.

2. Aside from the meat and oil, combine all ingredients thoroughly. Stir in the cooked onions, slowly without crumbling the meat further.

3. Make 8 patties and line them up on a baking tray (keep in the fridge for 30 minutes for best result).

4. Get them nicely golden and crispy, in 2 teaspoons of oil. Both sides will take about 3-5 minutes.

5. Serve!

Keto Lasagna from Scratch

Prep Time:	5 minutes	Calories:	241
Cook Time:	25 minutes	**Fat (g):**	25
Total Time:	30 minutes	**Protein (g):**	18
Servings:	4	**Net carbs (g):**	7

Ingredients:

- Edam cheese   7.05 oz. (10 thin slices)
- Butter   1 tablespoon

For Bolognese sauce:

- Olive oil   1 tablespoon
- Ground/minced beef   14 oz.
- Onion   1
- Garlic powder   ¼ teaspoon
- Sugar-free tomato sauce   ⅔ cup
- Sea salt   1 teaspoon
- Freshly ground pepper   to taste
- Oregano   1 teaspoon
- Dry basil   1 teaspoon

For ricotta filling:

- Ricotta cheese   8.81 oz.
- Eggs   2
- Salt   pinch
- Pepper   pinch

For cheese topping:

- Mozzarella   7 oz.
- Parmesan/ Grana padano cheese   0.7 oz.

Instructions:

1. Sauté the onions in olive oil until they turn translucent and brownish, then stir in the beef along with salt.

2. Cook till the juices are gone, and the beef turns brown. Then pour in tomato sauce and sprinkle ground pepper, garlic, oregano and basil. Mix well.

3. When the sauce starts to really thicken, turn off the heat.

4. For ricotta cheese filling, season the cheese with salt, some ground pepper, and crack eggs. Mix till no lumps are seen.

5. Grease the baking tray butter and thinly spread it with the ricotta filling, top with Edam cheese. Then goes the Bolognese and again more of ricotta filling.

6. Spread the Edam cheese and repeat process.

7. Lastly, a layer of parmesan cheese before setting the dish in the oven on 360C for 5 minutes.

8. When the cheese melts and becomes bubbly, remove from the oven. Serve hot!

Omelet pizza

Prep Time:	5 minutes	Calories:	368
Cook Time:	10 minutes	Fat (g):	27.5
Total Time:	15 minutes	Protein (g):	26.5
Servings:	2	Net carbs (g):	3.6

Ingredients:

- Lard of butter — 1 tablespoon
- Bacon or pancetta slices — 3.5 oz.
- Eggs — 4
- Mozzarella shredded — ½ cup
- Almond flour — 2 tablespoons
- Sea salt — 1 pinch
- Pepper — to taste
- **Toppings:** Basil (dried or fresh) — 1 pinch
- Dried oregano — 1 pinch
- Cherry tomatoes — 7 oz.
- Parmesan — 1 tablespoon

Instructions:

1. Spread the butter in a pan and sear bacon slices till they become crackly.
2. Take them out, add more lard in pan.
3. Whip eggs with salt, pepper, and flour. Add shredded mozzarella until the mixture does not look separated.
4. Place it on the heated pan for 7-8 minutes, simmer. When it's done, sprinkle 2 tablespoons of mozzarella and 1 tablespoon of parmesan. Toss in some cherry tomatoes and bacon with a dash of dried basils.
5. Serve!

Hassleback Chicken Caprese

Prep Time:	10 minutes	Calories:	552
Cook Time:	20 minutes	Fat (g):	27.21
Total Time:	30 minutes	Protein (g):	67.78
Servings:	2	Net carbs (g):	5.29

Ingredients:

- Skinless chicken breasts   2
- Homemade pesto   2 tablespoons
- Tomato   1
- Black olives   10
- Fresh goat mozzarella cheese   3.5 oz.
- Fresh basil   30 leaves
- Himalayan salt   ¼ teaspoon
- Black pepper   ¼ teaspoon
- Extra virgin olive oil   1 tablespoon

Instructions:

1. Heat the oven to 400F, beforehand.
2. Cut the tomatoes into two and divide each bit in half, as well as the olives. Divide the mozzarella into thin portions.
3. Make 1 cm wide ridges in the chicken.
4. Press a glob of pesto inside each ridge and then fill it with cheese, olives, tomatoes, and basil.
5. Drizzle oil in a skillet and line up the chicken gently onto it. Season with salt and pepper. Set in oven for 20 minutes.
6. Get your utensils ready for a hearty meal!

Italian Chicken Cacciatore

Prep Time:	10 minutes	Calories:	312
Cook Time:	20 minutes	Fat (g):	14
Total Time:	30 minutes	Protein (g):	34
Servings:	6	Net carbs (g):	7

Ingredients:

• Boneless-skinless chicken breast	2 lbs
• Sliced mushrooms	8 oz.
• Green bell pepper	4 oz.
• Red bell pepper	4 oz.
• Onion	4 oz.
• Garlic	2 cloves
• Garlic and herb seasoning	1 tablespoon
• Sherry	⅓ cup
• Chicken broth	1 cup
• Olive oil	⅓ cup
• Salt	¼ teaspoon
• Cornstarch	2 teaspoons
• Water	2 teaspoons

Instructions:

1. Cut the chicken into two, vertically. Slice them likewise. Rub them with 1 tablespoon of olive oil and 1 tablespoon of garlic and herb seasoning.
2. Grease the pan with olive oil. Over medium flame, sauté all the meat strips in batches until golden and done. Dish out.

3. Sauté the mushrooms after adding more oil and mix them in the chicken. Meanwhile, cut all the veggies into thin strands. Add them in after the mushrooms have been removed.

4. As soon as the veggies begin to absorb the leftover grease in the pan, add in chicken broth. Sherry goes in next. Mix well till nothing is stuck to the pan.

5. Toss in the chicken and mushrooms. Place the lid and let them sizzle. Make a concoction with 2 teaspoons each of cornstarch and water. Waste no time in mixing it in.

6. Then in goes a pinch of salt. Give the mixture a minute to reach desired consistency.

7. The fun part is here: serve!

Bacon Cheeseburger Soup

Prep Time:	5 minutes	Calories:	432.3
Cook Time:	15 minutes	**Fat (g):**	35
Total Time:	20 minutes	**Protein (g):**	25.7
Servings:	6	**Net carbs (g):**	3.8

Ingredients:

• Bacon	5 slices
• Ground beef	12 oz.
• Butter	2 tablespoons
• Beef broth	3 cups
• Garlic powder	½ teaspoon
• Onion powder	½ teaspoon
• Yellow mustard	2 teaspoons
• Black pepper	½ teaspoon
• Ground red pepper	½ teaspoon
• Cumin	1 teaspoon
• Chili powder	1 teaspoon
• Tomato paste	2 ½ tablespoons
• Diced dill pickle	1 medium
• Shredded cheddar cheese	1 cup
• Cream cheese	3 oz.
• Heavy cream	½ cup

Instructions:

1. Begin by frying the bacon in a pan.
2. Remove, after its brown and crisp. Add the hamburger meat in the same pan with its leftover grease.

3. Grease another pan with butter and stir in all the spices, for 45 seconds.

4. Pour the broth in with cheese, tomato paste, mustard, cream cheese, and let it be for 5 minutes till it's fully combined and smooth.

5. Glaze the cooked meat and crispy bacon with the whole sauce, cook on low flame for 5-10 minutes.

6. It is ready to eat!

Chicken Satay with Peanut Sauce

Prep Time:	15 minutes	Calories:	330
Cook Time:	15 minutes	Fat (g):	20
Total Time:	30 minutes	Protein (g):	30
Servings:	4	Net carbs (g):	3

Ingredients:

- Boneless-skinless chicken breasts   2
- Wooden skewers (soak for at least 30 minutes before using)   10
- Scallion (narrow slices)   1
- **Marinade:** Full-fat coconut milk   ½ cup
- Crushed garlic   3 cloves
- Curry powder   ½ teaspoon
- Salt   ½ teaspoon
- Ground black pepper   ½ teaspoon
- Cayenne powder   ¼ teaspoon
- **Peanut sauce:** Natural creamy peanut butter   ¼ cup
- Crushed garlic   3 cloves
- Sesame oil   2 tablespoons
- Olive oil   1 tablespoon
- Soy sauce   1 tablespoon
- Lime juice   1 tablespoon

Instructions:

1. In a mixing bowl, stir in all the marinade ingredients thoroughly. Slice the chicken into 1-inch cubes and fold them into the marinade, properly. Set in the refrigerator for 6 hours, at least.

2. Line the chicken bits onto the skewer until there is some space left to hold them. Set them in a single line on a huge baking tray. Set in the oven for 10 minutes at 450F. Turn them over and cook for 5 minutes more. You can also grill them instead of baking.

3. Meanwhile, combine all the peanut sauce ingredients in a pan, on medium-low flame. Simmer and stir till everything combines properly.

4. Dish out the skewers and glaze them with peanut sauce. Garnish with scallions and sprinkle black pepper. Bon appetite!

Spicy Ramen Bowl

Prep Time:	5 minutes	Calories:	103
Cook Time:	25 minutes	Fat (g):	3
Total Time:	30 minutes	Protein (g):	12
Servings:	5	Net carbs (g):	7

Ingredients:

- Olive oil   1 tablespoon

- Small Onion   1
- Freshly grated ginger   1 tablespoon
- Finely crushed garlic   3 cloves
- Chili paste   1 teaspoon
- Salt   ½ teaspoon
- Pepper   ¼ teaspoon
- Fish sauce   1 tablespoon
- Soy sauce/coconut aminos   ¼ cup
- Rice wine vinegar   ¼ cup
- Mushrooms, sliced thin   4 oz.
- Hard-boiled eggs   4
- Packed shirataki/zucchini noodles   2-3 packs or 4-5 cups respectively
- Bone broth   5 cups

Instructions:

1. In a huge stew pot, soften onions in oil for about 2-5 minutes, over medium flame.
2. Aside fork the eggs and noodles, stir in the rest of the ingredients. Keep the flame on low medium.
3. Run cold water over noodles.
4. Season the soup to taste.
5. Pour in the soup and noodles into bowls. Garnish with hard-boiled eggs, meat slices, sesame seeds, green onions and chili sauce (if you like it spicy).

Vegetarian Tikka Masala

Prep Time:	20 minutes	Calories:	248
Cook Time:	15 minutes	Fat (g):	21.2
Total Time:	30 minutes	Protein (g):	4.7
Servings:	5	Net carbs (g):	8

Ingredients:

- For Cauliflower: Florets   1.4 lbs
- Ground cumin   1 teaspoon
- Garam masala   1 teaspoon
- Cayenne pepper   ½ teaspoon
- Salt   ½ teaspoon
- Olive oil   1 tablespoon
- **Sauce:** Unsalted butter   4 tablespoons
- White onion, cubes   ½
- Crushed garlic   2 cloves
- Finely grated ginger   1 tablespoon
- Garam masala   1 tablespoon
- Paprika   1 ½ teaspoons
- Ground cumin   1 teaspoon
- Cayenne pepper   ½ teaspoon
- Salt   ½ teaspoon
- Coconut cream/heavy whipping cream   ½ cup
- Crushed cilantro   ¼ cup
- Minced tomatoes   1 ½ cups
- Water   1 cup

Instructions:

1. Heat the oven to 220C/425F, beforehand. Cover the florets with oil and spices in a mixing bowl. Line them up on a baking tray covered with foil. Set in the oven for 30 minutes until soft.

2. Before the rest of the 15 minutes are up, melt butter in a pot over medium-high flame. Sauté the onion, garlic and ginger for 5 minutes or till the onions turn brown.

3. Stir in the spices for 30 seconds. Mix in the tomatoes along with cream and water. Bring it to a light boil, keep stirring for 10 minutes.

4. Toss in the cauliflower and cilantro. Mix well

5. It is ready to be served!

Vegetarian Greek Collard Wraps

Prep Time:	30 minutes	Calories:	165
Cook Time:	0 minutes	Fat (g):	11.2
Total Time:	30 minutes	Protein (g):	6.9
Servings:	4	Net carbs (g):	7.3

Ingredients:

- **Tzatziki sauce:** Full-fat plain Greek   1 cup
  yogurt

• Garlic powder	1 teaspoon
• White vinegar	1 tablespoon
• Olive oil	2 tablespoons
• Cucumber, without seeds and shredded	2.5 oz.
• Crushed fresh dill	2 tablespoons
• Salt and pepper	to taste
• **The wraps:** Large Collard green leaves	4
• Cucumber, julienned	1
• Medium red bell pepper, julienned	½
• Purple onion, cubed	½
• Whole Kalamata olives, halved	8
• Block feta, cut into 4	½
• Large cherry tomatoes, halved	4

Instructions:

1. Whisk all the ingredients for the tzatziki sauce, the cucumbers should be soaked of all moisture.
2. Run the trimmed collard leaves underwater.
3. Place a layer of sauce in the middle of the wraps.
4. Line up all the veggies on top of the sauce layer.
5. Roll it up like a burrito and divide it into two. Serve with the sauce on the side.

Beef and Broccoli Bowls with Sunshine Sauce

Prep Time:	10 minutes	Calories:	388
Cook Time:	20 minutes	Fat (g):	29
Total Time:	30 minutes	Protein (g):	30
Servings:	4	Net carbs (g):	14

Ingredients:

- **Beef:** Cooking fat   1 tablespoon
- Lean pasteurized ground beef   1 lb
- Fine salt   1 teaspoon
- Minced garlic   1 teaspoon
- Coconut aminos   1 tablespoon
- **Broccoli:** Broccoli florets   4 crowns
- Avocado oil   1 tablespoon
- Fine salt   ½ teaspoon
- **Sunshine sauce:** Cooking fat   1 tablespoon
- Sunflower seed butter   2 tablespoons
- Bone broth   ¼ cup
- Crushed ginger   1 teaspoon
- Fine salt   ½ teaspoon
- Coconut aminos   2 teaspoon
- Lemon juice   1 lemon
- Minced green onion   1
- Baby spinach (optional-garnish)   4 cups

Instructions:

1. Heat the oven to 400F, beforehand.

2. Rub the broccoli with oil and fine salt, layer them out (at a little distance from each other) on the sheet pan. Set in the oven for 20 minutes.

3. Meanwhile, grease a sizeable, warm pot with fat. Break the ground beef into it and sprinkle in salt and garlic. Cook it till it's caramelized before stirring in the coconut aminos. Raise the flame to high.

4. Continue to stir until it becomes a darker shade and starts crackling.

5. As the beef cooks, put another small pan on medium flame and grease it with fat and sunflower seed butter next till it smoothens out.

6. Stir in the bone broth, ground ginger, salt, and aminos until it's mixed properly. Squeeze in the lemon juice after turning off the heat. Stir some more and add green onion. Keep aside.

7. Layer bowls with spinach, then beef, broccoli, and a generous heap of sauce. Enjoy!

Loaded Cauliflower Mash

Prep Time:	10 minutes	Calories:	199
Cook Time:	10 minutes	Fat (g):	17
Total Time:	20 minutes	Protein (g):	8
Servings:	6	Net carbs (g):	3

Ingredients:

• Cauliflower florets	1 lb
• Sour cream	4 oz.
• Cheddar cheese, grated	1 cup
• Cooked bacon, crushed	2 slices
• Snipped chives	2 tablespoons
• Butter	3 tablespoons
• Garlic powder	¼ teaspoon
• Salt and pepper	To taste

Instructions:

1. Add 2 tablespoons of water to the florets, wrap the microwave-safe bowl in cling film and set inside for 5-8 minutes or until they are soft and done. Remove and let them steam in the bowl for 2 minutes.

2. Pulp them in the food processor. Mix in the butter, sour cream, and garlic powder. Keep the processor running until its well-combined into a paste. Scrape it out and toss in the chives, save some for later use. Mix in the cheddar with your hand and sprinkle in salt and pepper.

3. Spread cheese over the cauliflower mix along with some olives and bacon. Microwave till the cheese melts.

4. Serve in cups and dig in!

Salmon Gremolata with vegetables

Prep Time:	10 minutes	Calories:	494
Cook Time:	20 minutes	Fat (g):	31
Total Time:	30 minutes	Protein (g):	42
Servings:	4	Net carbs (g):	7

Ingredients:

• Salmon fillets	4
• **Gremolata:** Garlic	2 cloves
• Parsley leaves	¼ cup
• Lemon zest	1 lemon
• Almond flour	1 cup
• Olive oil	1 tablespoon
• Salt and pepper	to taste
• **Roasted vegetables (optional):** Asparagus	1 bunch
• Cherry tomato	1
• Olive oil	1 tablespoon
• Salt and pepper	to taste

Instructions:

1. Preheat oven to 350F.
2. For the gremolata, blend all the ingredients together.
3. Line up the fillets on a baking tray covered with parchment or grease. Sprinkle salt and pepper and glaze them with oil. Scoop some gremolata and set it on top of the fillet.
4. If you want vegetables on the side, place them alongside the fillets after covering them with oil and a dash of salt and pepper.
5. Set in the oven for 15-20 minutes until the fish is done and golden. Enjoy!

Cauliflower Bibimbap

Prep Time:	15 minutes	Calories:	306
Cook Time:	15 minutes	Fat (g):	19
Total Time:	30 minutes	Protein (g):	14
Servings:	2	Net carbs (g):	14

Ingredients:

- Cauliflower — 1 head
- Kale — 2 cups
- Carrot (skinned and cut into thin strips) — 1
- Shitake mushroom slices — 6 oz.
- Bean sprouts — 1 cup
- Fresh baby spinach — 2 cups
- Eggs — 2
- Low-sodium soy sauce — 2 tablespoons
- Sesame oil — 2 tablespoons
- Sriracha — 2 tablespoons
- Salt and pepper — to taste
- Sesame seeds — for garnish

Instructions:

1. For cauliflower rice. Cut into small pieces and put them in a food processor. Scrape it into a bowl, place a paper towel on top and set it in the microwave for 4 minutes.

2. Toss the bean sprouts in a small pot of boiling water. Stir in 1 tablespoon each of sriracha and sesame oil and sesame seeds. Keep aside.

3. Repeat the same process when boiling the carrots.

4. Add 1 tablespoon of oil in a pan and tenderize the mushrooms. Pour 1 tablespoon of soy sauce on them and keep aside.

5. In the same pan, sauté the spinach until tender. Pour in some soy sauce and set aside. Do the kales in the same way.

6. Fry the egg.

7. Spread cauliflower into a bowl, the veggies and finally the egg on top. Drizzle sriracha or sausage. Mix everything and dig in!

Avocado Breakfast Burgers

Prep Time:	15 minutes	Calories:	657
Cook Time:	5 minutes	Fat (g):	121
Total Time:	20 minutes	Protein (g):	84
Servings:	1	Net carbs (g):	6

Ingredients:

- Ripe Avocado   1
- Egg   1
- Bacon rashers   2
- Red onion, sliced   1
- Tomato, sliced   1
- Lettuce leaf   1
- Paleo Mayonnaise   1 tablespoon
- Sea salt   To taste
- Sesame seeds   Garnish

Instructions:

1. On a cool frying pan, lay the bacon strips and turn on the heat. When they begin to crack, turn it off.
2. Dish the bacon out, and fry an egg in the bacon grease. Cook it sunny-side up.
3. Cut the avocado in half and remove its flesh.
4. Stuff the scooped out avocado with mayo, lettuce, tomato, onion, bacon and lastly, the egg.
5. Sprinkle sea salt.
6. Cover it with the other avocado part.
7. Garnish with sesame seeds. Have a happy breakfast!

Taco Bites

Prep Time:	15 minutes	Calories:	70
Cook Time:	15 minutes	Fat (g):	5
Total Time:	30 minutes	Protein (g):	4
Servings:	36	Net carbs (g):	1

Ingredients:

- Ground beef   1 lb
- Taco seasoning   2 ½-3 tablespoons
- Eggs   6 large
- Mexican blend shredded cheese (two bowls)   6 oz.
- Salsa, guacamole, olives, sour cream   for garnish

Instructions:

1. Cover muffin tin with muffin cups or grease with butter. Heat the oven to 350F, beforehand.
2. Sauté the beef over medium flame, until brown. Sprinkle in taco seasoning and cook it completely. Remove and let it come to room temperature.
3. Beat eggs in a bowl, stir in the meat, and 4 ounces of cheese. Pour the filling in the muffin liners and top it with the leftover cheese.
4. Set in the oven for 15-20 minutes until they rise up and become golden. Cool for ten minutes and serve with your favorite garnish!

Fried Chicken Tenders

Prep Time:	10 minutes	Calories:	193.6
Cook Time:	15 minutes	Fat (g):	9
Total Time:	25 minutes	Protein (g):	26.8
Servings:	8	Net carbs (g):	0.5

Ingredients:

- **Tenders:** Chicken tenders   8
- Jar of dill pickles   24 oz.
- Almond flour   ¾ cup
- Salt   1 teaspoon
- Pepper   1 teaspoon
- Eggs, whisked   2
- Pork panko   1 ½ cups
- Coconut oil   for frying
- **Sauce:** Mayonnaise   ½ cup
- Yellow mustard   2 teaspoons
- Lemon juice   1 teaspoon
- Sugar-free honey   2 teaspoons
- BBQ Sauce   1 tablespoon

Instructions:

1. Marinate the tenders with the dill juice, overnight for the best results. If not, for an hour at least.
2. Combine the flour, salt, and pepper into a mixing bowl.
3. Set three bowls in a line. One with the flour mix, the next with eggs, and the last one with pork panko.

4. Dip the tenders in the flour, eggs and lastly in the pork panko to coat them nicely.

5. Bring oil to the temperature of 350F, on medium-high flame.

6. Fry the tenders for 3 minutes on both sides.

7. Make the sauce by mixing in the ingredients.

8. Serve with a generous side of sauce.

Seared Scallops and Cauliflower Rice Risotto

Prep Time:	10 minutes	Calories:	551
Cook Time:	20 minutes	Fat (g):	47
Total Time:	30 minutes	Protein (g):	23
Servings:	4	Net carbs (g):	8

Ingredients:

- **Seared Scallops:** Jumbo Scallops — 1 lb
- Salted butter — 2 tablespoons
- Olive oil — 1 tablespoon
- Salt and pepper — To taste
- **Cauliflower risotto:** Riced cauliflower — 1 lb
- Salted butter — 3 tablespoons
- Crushed garlic cloves — 3 cloves
- Broccoli florets — 1 cup
- Green onions, thin slices — ¼ cup
- Heavy whipping cream — 1 cup
- Parmesan cheese grated — ¾ cup
- Sea salt — ¼ teaspoon
- Black pepper — ¼ teaspoon

Instructions:

1. Set a pot on medium flame, and grease with butter. Mix garlic, broccoli florets, and green onions into it. Stir until the broccoli becomes shiny green, for 3 minutes.
2. Stir in the rice till its almost soft for 3 minutes.

3. Mix in the rest of the ingredients until the cheese melts and it's well-combined. Cook on low heat till the rice is cooked through. Remove from the stove.

4. Season the scallops with salt and pepper.

5. Simmer butter and olive oil, on medium flame in a pan. Saute the scallops from both sides for 2 minutes. Dish out with a heap of risotto topped with scallops, green onions, and melted butter for a fancy touch.

Printed in Great Britain
by Amazon

45318691R00068